At School I Love to Meditate!

May your life be filled with peace & happiness

Max Matles

Dedicated to my loving parents Holly and David,
and everyone walking the path of peace.

With much love,

Max Matles

At school
I love to meditate
just breathing
in and out,

it helps me feel such
calm and peace
when others
yell or shout.

Calm
&
Peace

To meditate,
I stop and sit,
to see just how I feel.

I feel my head
down to my toes.
It helps my mind to
heal.

When days are good I
stop and sit
or even when I'm
naughty.

My head, my arms,
my legs, my feet,
I stop...
and feel my body.

When I have time I focus on just how my body feels.

I can do this anytime, before or after meals!

If times get really hard and I start to feel upset,

I can use my breath!

It's always with me!

I will not forget!

On sunny days my class and I will meditate together.

We sit outside on the grass and we enjoy the weather.

When we can’t
be at school and we
meditate alone,

this gives us the
chance to spread
peace within our
home.

Awareness of my breathing helps focus my mind,

and helps me see how others feel,

and helps me be more kind.

Everyone I know
and love,
they breathe and feel
like me!

When I feel great I
love to think…
“May we all be
happy!”

May everyone
be happy

Sharing thoughts of
love and peace
is my other
meditation,

I share them with the
whole wide world
and share them with
my nation!

I start by sharing thoughts of love with people that I know.

Then I share with everyone and let my kindness grow!

I share my thoughts of happiness with everyone I like.

Then I share with everyone, even Joe who took my bike!

Starting with the ones
I love,
I share my bliss with
all the others.

This helps me see all
those on Earth
as sisters and as
brothers.

I share my peace and happiness which helps me feel so free!

It also helps remind me that everyone is like me!

When I am happy
I share love
even with the trees,

with animals and
plants and people
I share my love for
free!

Every day is another chance to find peace using my breath,

It also helps prepare me for whatever may be next…

Meditation even helps me when it's time to go to bed!

My body feels relaxed and calm from my toes up to my head.

Next time I don't feel so well, here's what I can do...

I’ll take a couple deep long breaths,

I might not feel so blue!

Even when I’m
feeling down,
or fall and bump
my knee,

it warms my heart to
know that others
share their happiness
with me!

Meditations by
Zen Master
Thich Naht Han

Breathing in I see myself as a flower.

Breathing out I feel fresh.

Breathing in I see myself
as still water.

Breathing out I reflect
things as they truly are.

Breathing in I see myself as a mountain.

Breathing out I feel solid.

Short Guided Meditation to Read to Kids

This guided meditation is intended to be read aloud for kids of all ages. If you are the one reading this meditation guide out loud, make sure to read slowly and clearly. Also, make sure to pause at the right times and give the meditators a moment to soak in what they are experiencing. Lastly, make sure to fill your words with love, kindness, and understanding! May this meditation guide serve you and your loved ones well!

“Let’s begin by gently closing the eyes and taking a few long deep breaths in through the nose and out through the mouth.

(Pause)

You’re doing great. Continue breathing slowly and deeply allowing yourself to relax more and more as you listen to these words.

(Pause)

We give so much attention to what goes on outside of our body, but right now we are going to take some time to focus inside of ourselves as we relax and get even more in tune with our body and our mind.

(Pause)

Imagine yourself going on an adventure into your body and mind to discover what type of breathing makes you feel your best.
How does your breathing feel right now?
Can you make your breathing more comfortable by breathing into the nose and out of the nose? How about into the nose and out of the mouth? Right now is the time to gently play with your breathing, and see what feels best.

(Pause)

Maybe for you it would feel comfortable breathing in short and breathing out long, or maybe it would feel better breathing in long and breathing out short. Try to be gentle with yourself as you explore your breathing. You just might be surprised how good you can make your body and your mind feel by finding your most comfortable breath.

(Pause)

Sometimes it is better to breathe in a way that makes you relax…especially if you are having trouble trying to calm down.
Other times it is better to breathe in a way that gives you more energy, especially if you are feeling tired.

(Pause)

What kind of breathing would be good for you right now? And remember as you go on your adventure to find the breathing that is best for you, you are always learning more about yourself with each breath, even if you get distracted sometimes. Imagine you are breathing air into your body from every direction, allowing the breath to fill your belly and spread to every cell of your body.

(Pause)

As you continue breathing comfortably, bring your attention to your face and try to relax your entire face. Start by relaxing your forehead, relaxing your eyebrows, relaxing your nose, your cheeks, your lips, your chin.
Try and see if you can relax your whole head. The sides of your head, the back of your head, and the front of your head.

(Pause)

Continue breathing and now bring your attention to your neck and try relaxing your neck, relaxing your throat, and then go down to your shoulders. It's okay if you get distracted, we all get distracted sometimes, just do your best to focus on your breath while spreading your awareness to each part of your body.

(Pause)

See if you can relax both of your arms, starting at the top of your arms…
then going down to your elbows, then to your wrists, then your hands, and then each of your fingers, even the tiniest part of your pinky finger.

(Pause)

Relax your chest, relax your belly, relax your back and now down to your legs, all the way down to the tops of your legs, down to your knees, to your feet, to your toes, and even your pinky toe.

(Pause)

How does your body feel now? Maybe you feel really calm, relaxed, and happy. Maybe you feel a little distracted and you don't feel your best right now, and that's ok.

However you feel right now, take a moment to silently wish yourself happiness. Let's take this time to silently say to ourselves, "May I be happy and peaceful".

(Pause)

Without answering out loud, how does it feel to wish happiness for yourself?

(Pause)

Let's take another deep calming breath and this time we will silently wish happiness for someone we love a lot. "May they be happy and share our peace."

(Pause)

Let's take just a few more deep breaths and silently wish happiness for ourselves, for each other, and everyone in the world, even the people we don't like.

May we all be happy and peaceful.

(Pause)

As you start to finish up this meditation you can slowly open your eyes. Silently ask yourself how does your body feel?
How does your breathing feel? Do you feel any different than when you started this meditation?

(Pause)

As we finish up, remember that you can always stop and take a few deep relaxing breaths wherever you are and whenever life feels hard.

(Pause)

This is the end of the meditation, you did a great job!

Meditation Resources for teachers, parents, adults, and kids:

AtSchoolILovetoMeditate.com

Children.dhamma.org

Classdojo.com

Mindful.org

GoNoodle.com

If you have any questions, comments, or feedback for this book or mindfulness for children in general, please feel free to reach out to the author Max Matles. If you are a teacher, parent, or loving adult interested in purchasing this book for your school or organization at discounted prices, please do not hesitate to contact:

AtSchoolILovetoMeditate@gmail.com

Additional resources for this book can be found at:

AtSchoolILovetoMeditate.com

ISBN: 9781638779742

Made in the USA
Columbia, SC
09 September 2021